Life can be stressful and filled with anxiety. But it is also filled with beauty, joy, and fulfillment. If you focus on the latter you will start noticing the stressful events less and begin enjoying every day more. Practicing gratitude is one of the simplest and most effective things you can do to transform your life.

Gratitude is appreciation for every moment in your life.
It is a feeling of thankfulness for the blessings we have received.

"Keeping a personal journal a daily in-depth analysis and evaluation of your experiences is a high-leverage activity that increases self-awareness and enhances all the endowments and the synergy among them."
                                    - Stephen R Covey

Daily Gratitude Journal
113 numbered pages - 120 total pages
Design © 2020 Blank Classics

Blank Classic

Mailing address:
Blank Classic
PO BOX 4608
Main Station Terminal
349 West Georgia Street
Vancouver, BC
Canada, V6B 4A1

Cover design by: Lauren Dick

ISBN: 978-1-77476-019-2

FIRST EDITION / FIRST PRINTING

Name _____

Address _____

_____

_____

_____

_____

GRATITUDE

MY WEEKLY GOALS ARE...

1. _____
2. _____
3. _____

I AM THANKFUL FOR...   DATE:

1. _____
2. _____
3. _____

I AM THANKFUL FOR...   DATE:

1. _____
2. _____
3. _____

I AM THANKFUL FOR...   DATE:

1. _____
2. _____
3. _____

"We can only be said to be alive in those moments when our hearts are conscious of our treasures."

Thornton Wilder

I AM THANKFUL FOR... DATE:

1.

2.

3.

I AM THANKFUL FOR... DATE:

1.

2.

3.

I AM THANKFUL FOR... DATE:

1.

2.

3.

I AM THANKFUL FOR... DATE:

1.

2.

3.

START YOUR DAY WITH

GRATITUDE

MY WEEKLY GOALS ARE...

1. _____
2. _____
3. _____

I AM THANKFUL FOR...   DATE:

1. _____
2. _____
3. _____

I AM THANKFUL FOR...   DATE:

1. _____
2. _____
3. _____

I AM THANKFUL FOR...   DATE:

1. _____
2. _____
3. _____

"Do not indulge in dreams of having what you have not, but reckon up the chief of the blessings you do possess, and then thankfully remember how you would crave for them if they were not yours."

Marcus Aurelius

I AM THANKFUL FOR... DATE:

1.

2.

3.

I AM THANKFUL FOR... DATE:

1.

2.

3.

I AM THANKFUL FOR... DATE:

1.

2.

3.

I AM THANKFUL FOR... DATE:

1.

2.

3.

START YOUR DAY WITH

GRATITUDE

MY WEEKLY GOALS ARE...

1. _____

2. _____

3. _____

I AM THANKFUL FOR...   DATE:

1. _____

2. _____

3. _____

I AM THANKFUL FOR...   DATE:

1. _____

2. _____

3. _____

I AM THANKFUL FOR...   DATE:

1. _____

2. _____

3. _____

> "Gratitude is not only the greatest of virtues, but the parent of all others."
>
> **Cicero**

I AM THANKFUL FOR...   DATE:

1.

2.

3.

I AM THANKFUL FOR...   DATE:

1.

2.

3.

I AM THANKFUL FOR...   DATE:

1.

2.

3.

I AM THANKFUL FOR...   DATE:

1.

2.

3.

GRATITUDE

MY WEEKLY GOALS ARE...

1. _____
2. _____
3. _____

I AM THANKFUL FOR...   DATE:

1. _____
2. _____
3. _____

I AM THANKFUL FOR...   DATE:

1. _____
2. _____
3. _____

I AM THANKFUL FOR...   DATE:

1. _____
2. _____
3. _____

"Be thankful for what you have; you'll end up having more. If you concentrate on what you don't have, you will never, ever have enough."

Oprah Winfrey

I AM THANKFUL FOR... DATE:

1.

2.

3.

I AM THANKFUL FOR... DATE:

1.

2.

3.

I AM THANKFUL FOR... DATE:

1.

2.

3.

I AM THANKFUL FOR... DATE:

1.

2.

3.

START YOUR DAY WITH

GRATITUDE

MY WEEKLY GOALS ARE...

1. _____

2. _____

3. _____

I AM THANKFUL FOR...................... DATE: ....

1. _____

2. _____

3. _____

I AM THANKFUL FOR...................... DATE: ....

1. _____

2. _____

3. _____

I AM THANKFUL FOR...................... DATE: ....

1. _____

2. _____

3. _____

"We would worry less if we praised more. Thanksgiving is the enemy of discontent and dissatisfaction."

H.A. Ironside

I AM THANKFUL FOR... DATE:

1.

2.

3.

I AM THANKFUL FOR... DATE:

1.

2.

3.

I AM THANKFUL FOR... DATE:

1.

2.

3.

I AM THANKFUL FOR... DATE:

1.

2.

3.

START YOUR DAY WITH

GRATITUDE

MY WEEKLY GOALS ARE...

1. _____
2. _____
3. _____

I AM THANKFUL FOR...   DATE:

1. _____
2. _____
3. _____

I AM THANKFUL FOR...   DATE:

1. _____
2. _____
3. _____

I AM THANKFUL FOR...   DATE:

1. _____
2. _____
3. _____

"The soul that gives thanks can find comfort in everything; the soul that complains can find comfort in nothing."

Hannah Whitall Smith

I AM THANKFUL FOR...   DATE:

1. _____

2. _____

3. _____

I AM THANKFUL FOR...   DATE:

1. _____

2. _____

3. _____

I AM THANKFUL FOR...   DATE:

1. _____

2. _____

3. _____

I AM THANKFUL FOR...   DATE:

1. _____

2. _____

3. _____

START YOUR DAY WITH

GRATITUDE

MY WEEKLY GOALS ARE...

1. _____

2. _____

3. _____

I AM THANKFUL FOR...   DATE:

1. _____

2. _____

3. _____

I AM THANKFUL FOR...   DATE:

1. _____

2. _____

3. _____

I AM THANKFUL FOR...   DATE:

1. _____

2. _____

3. _____

"Dwell on the beauty of life. Watch the stars, and see yourself running with them."

Marcus Aurelius

I AM THANKFUL FOR...   DATE:

1.

2.

3.

I AM THANKFUL FOR...   DATE:

1.

2.

3.

I AM THANKFUL FOR...   DATE:

1.

2.

3.

I AM THANKFUL FOR...   DATE:

1.

2.

3.

START YOUR DAY WITH

GRATITUDE

MY WEEKLY GOALS ARE...

1. _____
2. _____
3. _____

I AM THANKFUL FOR...   DATE:

1. _____
2. _____
3. _____

I AM THANKFUL FOR...   DATE:

1. _____
2. _____
3. _____

I AM THANKFUL FOR...   DATE:

1. _____
2. _____
3. _____

"Cultivate the habit of being grateful for every good thing that comes to you, and to give thanks continuously. And because all things have contributed to your advancement, you should include all things in your gratitude."

Ralph Waldo Emerson

I AM THANKFUL FOR...   DATE:

1.

2.

3.

I AM THANKFUL FOR...   DATE:

1.

2.

3.

I AM THANKFUL FOR...   DATE:

1.

2.

3.

I AM THANKFUL FOR...   DATE:

1.

2.

3.

COME TOGETHER IN

REFLECTION

TAKE THE TIME TO LOOK BACK OVER TO PAST WEEKS AND REFLECT ON WHAT YOU WERE THANKFUL FOR, THE WAY IT MADE YOU FEEL AND HOW YOU FEEL NOW! SET SOME NEW MONTHLY GOALS THAT WILL PUSH YOU TO BE THE BEST VERSION OF YOURSELF.

MY GOALS FOR THE MONTH ARE...

1. _____

2. _____

3. _____

4. _____

5. _____

WHAT HAVE I BEEN MOST GRATEFUL FOR...

_____

_____

_____

_____

_____

_____

_____

_____

_____

Draw Something

START YOUR DAY WITH

GRATITUDE

MY WEEKLY GOALS ARE...

1.

2.

3.

I AM THANKFUL FOR...   DATE:

1.

2.

3.

I AM THANKFUL FOR...   DATE:

1.

2.

3.

I AM THANKFUL FOR...   DATE:

1.

2.

3.

"To witness miracles unfold in your experience, count your blessings and be thankful. Perceived small blessings accumulate to be the most powerful."

T.F. Hodge

I AM THANKFUL FOR...   DATE:

1.

2.

3.

I AM THANKFUL FOR...   DATE:

1.

2.

3.

I AM THANKFUL FOR...   DATE:

1.

2.

3.

I AM THANKFUL FOR...   DATE:

1.

2.

3.

START YOUR DAY WITH

GRATITUDE

MY WEEKLY GOALS ARE...

1. _____

2. _____

3. _____

I AM THANKFUL FOR...   DATE:

1. _____

2. _____

3. _____

I AM THANKFUL FOR...   DATE:

1. _____

2. _____

3. _____

I AM THANKFUL FOR...   DATE:

1. _____

2. _____

3. _____

"Sometimes we focus so much on what we don't have that we fail to see, appreciate, and use what we do have!"

Jeff Dixon

I AM THANKFUL FOR...   DATE:

1.

2.

3.

I AM THANKFUL FOR...   DATE:

1.

2.

3.

I AM THANKFUL FOR...   DATE:

1.

2.

3.

I AM THANKFUL FOR...   DATE:

1.

2.

3.

START YOUR DAY WITH

GRATITUDE

MY WEEKLY GOALS ARE...

1. _____
2. _____
3. _____

I AM THANKFUL FOR...   DATE:

1. _____
2. _____
3. _____

I AM THANKFUL FOR...   DATE:

1. _____
2. _____
3. _____

I AM THANKFUL FOR...   DATE:

1. _____
2. _____
3. _____

"The invariable mark of wisdom is to see the miraculous in the common."

Ralph Waldo Emerson

I AM THANKFUL FOR...   DATE:

1. _____

2. _____

3. _____

I AM THANKFUL FOR...   DATE:

1. _____

2. _____

3. _____

I AM THANKFUL FOR...   DATE:

1. _____

2. _____

3. _____

I AM THANKFUL FOR...   DATE:

1. _____

2. _____

3. _____

START YOUR DAY WITH

GRATITUDE

MY WEEKLY GOALS ARE...

1. _____
2. _____
3. _____

I AM THANKFUL FOR...   DATE:

1. _____
2. _____
3. _____

I AM THANKFUL FOR...   DATE:

1. _____
2. _____
3. _____

I AM THANKFUL FOR...   DATE:

1. _____
2. _____
3. _____

"Sometimes we spend so much time and energy thinking about where we want to go that we don't notice where we happen to be."

Dan Gutman

I AM THANKFUL FOR...   DATE:

1.

2.

3.

I AM THANKFUL FOR...   DATE:

1.

2.

3.

I AM THANKFUL FOR...   DATE:

1.

2.

3.

I AM THANKFUL FOR...   DATE:

1.

2.

3.

START YOUR DAY WITH

GRATITUDE

MY WEEKLY GOALS ARE...

1. _____
2. _____
3. _____

I AM THANKFUL FOR...   DATE:

1. _____
2. _____
3. _____

I AM THANKFUL FOR...   DATE:

1. _____
2. _____
3. _____

I AM THANKFUL FOR...   DATE:

1. _____
2. _____
3. _____

You simply will not be the same person two months from now after consciously giving thanks each day for the abundance that exists in your life. And you will have set in motion an ancient spiritual law: the more you have and are grateful for, the more will be given you."

Sarah Ban Breathnach

I AM THANKFUL FOR...   DATE:

1.

2.

3.

I AM THANKFUL FOR...   DATE:

1.

2.

3.

I AM THANKFUL FOR...   DATE:

1.

2.

3.

I AM THANKFUL FOR...   DATE:

1.

2.

3.

START YOUR DAY WITH

GRATITUDE

MY WEEKLY GOALS ARE...

1. _____
2. _____
3. _____

I AM THANKFUL FOR...   DATE:

1. _____
2. _____
3. _____

I AM THANKFUL FOR...   DATE:

1. _____
2. _____
3. _____

I AM THANKFUL FOR...   DATE:

1. _____
2. _____
3. _____

> "We pray for the big things and forget to give thanks for the ordinary, small (and yet really not small) gifts."
>
> **Dietrich Bonhoeffer**

I AM THANKFUL FOR...   DATE:

1.

2.

3.

I AM THANKFUL FOR...   DATE:

1.

2.

3.

I AM THANKFUL FOR...   DATE:

1.

2.

3.

I AM THANKFUL FOR...   DATE:

1.

2.

3.

GRATITUDE

MY WEEKLY GOALS ARE...

1. _____
2. _____
3. _____

I AM THANKFUL FOR...   DATE:

1. _____
2. _____
3. _____

I AM THANKFUL FOR...   DATE:

1. _____
2. _____
3. _____

I AM THANKFUL FOR...   DATE:

1. _____
2. _____
3. _____

"In order to complete our amazing life journey successfully, it is vital that we turn each and every dark tear into a pearl of wisdom, and find the blessing in every curse."

Anthon St. Maarten

I AM THANKFUL FOR...   DATE:

1.

2.

3.

I AM THANKFUL FOR...   DATE:

1.

2.

3.

I AM THANKFUL FOR...   DATE:

1.

2.

3.

I AM THANKFUL FOR...   DATE:

1.

2.

3.

START YOUR DAY WITH

GRATITUDE

MY WEEKLY GOALS ARE...

1. _____

2. _____

3. _____

I AM THANKFUL FOR...   DATE:

1. _____

2. _____

3. _____

I AM THANKFUL FOR...   DATE:

1. _____

2. _____

3. _____

I AM THANKFUL FOR...   DATE:

1. _____

2. _____

3. _____

"Whatever happens in your life, no matter how troubling things might seem, do not enter the neighborhood of despair. Even when all doors remain closed, God will open up a new path only for you. Be thankful!"

Elif Shafak

I AM THANKFUL FOR...   DATE:

1.

2.

3.

I AM THANKFUL FOR...   DATE:

1.

2.

3.

I AM THANKFUL FOR...   DATE:

1.

2.

3.

I AM THANKFUL FOR...   DATE:

1.

2.

3.

COME TOGETHER IN

REFLECTION

TAKE THE TIME TO LOOK BACK OVER TO PAST WEEKS AND
REFLECT ON WHAT YOU WERE THANKFUL FOR, THE WAY IT
MADE YOU FEEL AND HOW YOU FEEL NOW! SET SOME NEW
MONTHLY GOALS THAT WILL PUSH YOU TO BE THE BEST
VERSION OF YOURSELF.

MY GOALS FOR THE MONTH ARE...

1. _____

2. _____

3. _____

4. _____

5. _____

WHAT HAVE I BEEN MOST GRATEFUL FOR...

_____

_____

_____

_____

_____

_____

_____

_____

Draw Something

START YOUR DAY WITH

GRATITUDE

MY WEEKLY GOALS ARE...

1. _____

2. _____

3. _____

I AM THANKFUL FOR...   DATE:

1. _____

2. _____

3. _____

I AM THANKFUL FOR...   DATE:

1. _____

2. _____

3. _____

I AM THANKFUL FOR...   DATE:

1. _____

2. _____

3. _____

"Do not spoil what you have by desiring what you have not; remember that what you now have was once among the things you only hoped for."

Epicurus

I AM THANKFUL FOR... DATE:

1.

2.

3.

I AM THANKFUL FOR... DATE:

1.

2.

3.

I AM THANKFUL FOR... DATE:

1.

2.

3.

I AM THANKFUL FOR... DATE:

1.

2.

3.

START YOUR DAY WITH

GRATITUDE

MY WEEKLY GOALS ARE...

1. _____

2. _____

3. _____

I AM THANKFUL FOR...   DATE:

1. _____

2. _____

3. _____

I AM THANKFUL FOR...   DATE:

1. _____

2. _____

3. _____

I AM THANKFUL FOR...   DATE:

1. _____

2. _____

3. _____

> "Some people grumble that roses have thorns; I am grateful
> that thorns have roses."
>
> **Alphonse Karr**

I AM THANKFUL FOR...   DATE:

1.

2.

3.

I AM THANKFUL FOR...   DATE:

1.

2.

3.

I AM THANKFUL FOR...   DATE:

1.

2.

3.

I AM THANKFUL FOR...   DATE:

1.

2.

3.

START YOUR DAY WITH

GRATITUDE

MY WEEKLY GOALS ARE...

1. _____

2. _____

3. _____

I AM THANKFUL FOR...   DATE:

1. _____

2. _____

3. _____

I AM THANKFUL FOR...   DATE:

1. _____

2. _____

3. _____

I AM THANKFUL FOR...   DATE:

1. _____

2. _____

3. _____

> "One of the main reasons that we lose our enthusiasm in life is because we become ungrateful... we let what was once a miracle become common to us. We get so accustomed to his goodness it becomes a routine."
>
> **Joel Osteen**

I AM THANKFUL FOR...   DATE:

1.

2.

3.

I AM THANKFUL FOR...   DATE:

1.

2.

3.

I AM THANKFUL FOR...   DATE:

1.

2.

3.

I AM THANKFUL FOR...   DATE:

1.

2.

3.

START YOUR DAY WITH

GRATITUDE

MY WEEKLY GOALS ARE...

1. _____

2. _____

3. _____

I AM THANKFUL FOR...   DATE:

1. _____

2. _____

3. _____

I AM THANKFUL FOR...   DATE:

1. _____

2. _____

3. _____

I AM THANKFUL FOR...   DATE:

1. _____

2. _____

3. _____

> "Acknowledging the good that you already have in your life is the foundation for all abundance."
>
> **Eckhart Tolle**

I AM THANKFUL FOR...   DATE:

1.

2.

3.

I AM THANKFUL FOR...   DATE:

1.

2.

3.

I AM THANKFUL FOR...   DATE:

1.

2.

3.

I AM THANKFUL FOR...   DATE:

1.

2.

3.

START YOUR DAY WITH

GRATITUDE

MY WEEKLY GOALS ARE...

1. _____

2. _____

3. _____

I AM THANKFUL FOR...   DATE:

1. _____

2. _____

3. _____

I AM THANKFUL FOR...   DATE:

1. _____

2. _____

3. _____

I AM THANKFUL FOR...   DATE:

1. _____

2. _____

3. _____

> "Life without thankfulness is devoid of love and passion. Hope without thankfulness is lacking in fine perception. Faith without thankfulness lacks strength and fortitude. Every virtue divorced from thankfulness is maimed and limps along the spiritual road."
>
> **John Henry Jowett**

I AM THANKFUL FOR...   DATE:

1.

2.

3.

I AM THANKFUL FOR...   DATE:

1.

2.

3.

I AM THANKFUL FOR...   DATE:

1.

2.

3.

I AM THANKFUL FOR...   DATE:

1.

2.

3.

START YOUR DAY WITH

GRATITUDE

MY WEEKLY GOALS ARE...

1. _____
2. _____
3. _____

I AM THANKFUL FOR...   DATE:

1. _____
2. _____
3. _____

I AM THANKFUL FOR...   DATE:

1. _____
2. _____
3. _____

I AM THANKFUL FOR...   DATE:

1. _____
2. _____
3. _____

> "Joy is thankfulness, and when we are joyful, that is the best expression of thanks we can offer the Lord, Who delivers us from sorrow and sin."
>
> **Thaddeus of Vitovnica**

I AM THANKFUL FOR...   DATE:

1.

2.

3.

I AM THANKFUL FOR...   DATE:

1.

2.

3.

I AM THANKFUL FOR...   DATE:

1.

2.

3.

I AM THANKFUL FOR...   DATE:

1.

2.

3.

GRATITUDE

MY WEEKLY GOALS ARE...

1.
2.
3.

I AM THANKFUL FOR...   DATE:

1.
2.
3.

I AM THANKFUL FOR...   DATE:

1.
2.
3.

I AM THANKFUL FOR...   DATE:

1.
2.
3.

"We can choose to be grateful no matter what."

Dieter F. Uchtdorf

I AM THANKFUL FOR... DATE:

1.

2.

3.

I AM THANKFUL FOR... DATE:

1.

2.

3.

I AM THANKFUL FOR... DATE:

1.

2.

3.

I AM THANKFUL FOR... DATE:

1.

2.

3.

GRATITUDE

MY WEEKLY GOALS ARE...

1. _____
2. _____
3. _____

I AM THANKFUL FOR...   DATE:

1. _____
2. _____
3. _____

I AM THANKFUL FOR...   DATE:

1. _____
2. _____
3. _____

I AM THANKFUL FOR...   DATE:

1. _____
2. _____
3. _____

"Act with kindness, but do not expect gratitude."

Confucius

I AM THANKFUL FOR... DATE:

1.

2.

3.

I AM THANKFUL FOR... DATE:

1.

2.

3.

I AM THANKFUL FOR... DATE:

1.

2.

3.

I AM THANKFUL FOR... DATE:

1.

2.

3.

REFLECTION

TAKE THE TIME TO LOOK BACK OVER TO PAST WEEKS AND REFLECT ON WHAT YOU WERE THANKFUL FOR, THE WAY IT MADE YOU FEEL AND HOW YOU FEEL NOW! SET SOME NEW MONTHLY GOALS THAT WILL PUSH YOU TO BE THE BEST VERSION OF YOURSELF.

MY GOALS FOR THE MONTH ARE...

1. _____
2. _____
3. _____
4. _____
5. _____

WHAT HAVE I BEEN MOST GRATEFUL FOR...

_____
_____
_____
_____
_____
_____
_____
_____
_____

Draw Something

START YOUR DAY WITH

GRATITUDE

MY WEEKLY GOALS ARE...

1. _____
2. _____
3. _____

I AM THANKFUL FOR...   DATE:

1. _____
2. _____
3. _____

I AM THANKFUL FOR...   DATE:

1. _____
2. _____
3. _____

I AM THANKFUL FOR...   DATE:

1. _____
2. _____
3. _____

"I've never before been so aware of the thousands of little good things, the thousands of things that go right every day."

A.J. Jacobs

I AM THANKFUL FOR... DATE:

1.

2.

3.

I AM THANKFUL FOR... DATE:

1.

2.

3.

I AM THANKFUL FOR... DATE:

1.

2.

3.

I AM THANKFUL FOR... DATE:

1.

2.

3.

START YOUR DAY WITH

GRATITUDE

MY WEEKLY GOALS ARE...

1. _____
2. _____
3. _____

I AM THANKFUL FOR...   DATE:

1. _____
2. _____
3. _____

I AM THANKFUL FOR...   DATE:

1. _____
2. _____
3. _____

I AM THANKFUL FOR...   DATE:

1. _____
2. _____
3. _____

"Gratitude paints little smiley faces on everything it touches."

Richelle E. Goodrich

I AM THANKFUL FOR... DATE:

1.

2.

3.

I AM THANKFUL FOR... DATE:

1.

2.

3.

I AM THANKFUL FOR... DATE:

1.

2.

3.

I AM THANKFUL FOR... DATE:

1.

2.

3.

GRATITUDE

MY WEEKLY GOALS ARE...

1. _____

2. _____

3. _____

I AM THANKFUL FOR...   DATE:

1. _____

2. _____

3. _____

I AM THANKFUL FOR...   DATE:

1. _____

2. _____

3. _____

I AM THANKFUL FOR...   DATE:

1. _____

2. _____

3. _____

"Be savagely thankful, and continuously in awe of the power you possess. You are alive. Inside of an endless cosmos with the freedom that shines brightest in the dark."

Shane L. Koyczan

I AM THANKFUL FOR... DATE:

1.

2.

3.

I AM THANKFUL FOR... DATE:

1.

2.

3.

I AM THANKFUL FOR... DATE:

1.

2.

3.

I AM THANKFUL FOR... DATE:

1.

2.

3.

GRATITUDE

MY WEEKLY GOALS ARE...

1. _____

2. _____

3. _____

I AM THANKFUL FOR...   DATE:

1. _____

2. _____

3. _____

I AM THANKFUL FOR...   DATE:

1. _____

2. _____

3. _____

I AM THANKFUL FOR...   DATE:

1. _____

2. _____

3. _____

"Let gratitude be the pillow upon which you kneel to say your nightly prayer. And let faith be the bridge you build to overcome evil and welcome good."

Maya Angelou

I AM THANKFUL FOR...   DATE:

1.

2.

3.

I AM THANKFUL FOR...   DATE:

1.

2.

3.

I AM THANKFUL FOR...   DATE:

1.

2.

3.

I AM THANKFUL FOR...   DATE:

1.

2.

3.

GRATITUDE

MY WEEKLY GOALS ARE...

1. _____
2. _____
3. _____

I AM THANKFUL FOR...   DATE:

1. _____
2. _____
3. _____

I AM THANKFUL FOR...   DATE:

1. _____
2. _____
3. _____

I AM THANKFUL FOR...   DATE:

1. _____
2. _____
3. _____

> "All happy people are grateful, and ungrateful people cannot be happy. Become grateful and you will become a much happier person."
>
> **Dennis Prager**

I AM THANKFUL FOR...   DATE:

1. _____
2. _____
3. _____

I AM THANKFUL FOR...   DATE:

1. _____
2. _____
3. _____

I AM THANKFUL FOR...   DATE:

1. _____
2. _____
3. _____

I AM THANKFUL FOR...   DATE:

1. _____
2. _____
3. _____

START YOUR DAY WITH

GRATITUDE

MY WEEKLY GOALS ARE...

1. _____
2. _____
3. _____

I AM THANKFUL FOR...   DATE:

1. _____
2. _____
3. _____

I AM THANKFUL FOR...   DATE:

1. _____
2. _____
3. _____

I AM THANKFUL FOR...   DATE:

1. _____
2. _____
3. _____

> "It is only normal that people count losses with their minds, and ignore to count blessings with the graciousness of their hearts."
>
> **Suzy Kassem**

I AM THANKFUL FOR...   DATE:

1.

2.

3.

I AM THANKFUL FOR...   DATE:

1.

2.

3.

I AM THANKFUL FOR...   DATE:

1.

2.

3.

I AM THANKFUL FOR...   DATE:

1.

2.

3.

GRATITUDE

MY WEEKLY GOALS ARE...

1. _____
2. _____
3. _____

I AM THANKFUL FOR...   DATE:

1. _____
2. _____
3. _____

I AM THANKFUL FOR...   DATE:

1. _____
2. _____
3. _____

I AM THANKFUL FOR...   DATE:

1. _____
2. _____
3. _____

> "Being grateful does not mean that everything is necessarily good. It just means that you can accept it as a gift."
>
> **Roy T. Bennett**

I AM THANKFUL FOR...   DATE:

1.

2.

3.

I AM THANKFUL FOR...   DATE:

1.

2.

3.

I AM THANKFUL FOR...   DATE:

1.

2.

3.

I AM THANKFUL FOR...   DATE:

1.

2.

3.

START YOUR DAY WITH

GRATITUDE

MY WEEKLY GOALS ARE...

1. _____

2. _____

3. _____

I AM THANKFUL FOR...   DATE:

1. _____

2. _____

3. _____

I AM THANKFUL FOR...   DATE:

1. _____

2. _____

3. _____

I AM THANKFUL FOR...   DATE:

1. _____

2. _____

3. _____

"Because thankfulness is the tonic that always cures the cancers of greed, envy and jealousy, it should be taken in liberal doses daily."

Craig D. Lounsbrough

I AM THANKFUL FOR...   DATE:

1.

2.

3.

I AM THANKFUL FOR...   DATE:

1.

2.

3.

I AM THANKFUL FOR...   DATE:

1.

2.

3.

I AM THANKFUL FOR...   DATE:

1.

2.

3.

COME TOGETHER IN

REFLECTION

TAKE THE TIME TO LOOK BACK OVER TO PAST WEEKS AND
REFLECT ON WHAT YOU WERE THANKFUL FOR, THE WAY IT
MADE YOU FEEL AND HOW YOU FEEL NOW! SET SOME NEW
MONTHLY GOALS THAT WILL PUSH YOU TO BE THE BEST
VERSION OF YOURSELF.

MY GOALS FOR THE MONTH ARE...

1. _____

2. _____

3. _____

4. _____

5. _____

WHAT HAVE I BEEN MOST GRATEFUL FOR...

_____

_____

_____

_____

_____

_____

_____

_____

_____

Draw Something

GRATITUDE

MY WEEKLY GOALS ARE...

1. _____

2. _____

3. _____

I AM THANKFUL FOR...   DATE:

1. _____

2. _____

3. _____

I AM THANKFUL FOR...   DATE:

1. _____

2. _____

3. _____

I AM THANKFUL FOR...   DATE:

1. _____

2. _____

3. _____

"Be grateful for what you already have while you pursue your goals. If you aren't grateful for what you already have, what makes you think you would be happy with more."

Roy T. Bennett

I AM THANKFUL FOR...   DATE:

1.

2.

3.

I AM THANKFUL FOR...   DATE:

1.

2.

3.

I AM THANKFUL FOR...   DATE:

1.

2.

3.

I AM THANKFUL FOR...   DATE:

1.

2.

3.

START YOUR DAY WITH

GRATITUDE

MY WEEKLY GOALS ARE...

1. _____

2. _____

3. _____

I AM THANKFUL FOR...   DATE:

1. _____

2. _____

3. _____

I AM THANKFUL FOR...   DATE:

1. _____

2. _____

3. _____

I AM THANKFUL FOR...   DATE:

1. _____

2. _____

3. _____

> "We find it hard to be thankful. To see the gift each day brings us. It is from this lack of true gratitude that we become sad."
>
> **S.R. Crawford**

I AM THANKFUL FOR... DATE:

1.

2.

3.

I AM THANKFUL FOR... DATE:

1.

2.

3.

I AM THANKFUL FOR... DATE:

1.

2.

3.

I AM THANKFUL FOR... DATE:

1.

2.

3.

START YOUR DAY WITH

GRATITUDE

MY WEEKLY GOALS ARE...

1. _____
2. _____
3. _____

I AM THANKFUL FOR...   DATE:

1. _____
2. _____
3. _____

I AM THANKFUL FOR...   DATE:

1. _____
2. _____
3. _____

I AM THANKFUL FOR...   DATE:

1. _____
2. _____
3. _____

> "To live, to truly live, one must consider each and every thing a blessing."
>
> **Kamand Kojouri**

I AM THANKFUL FOR...   DATE:

1.
2.
3.

I AM THANKFUL FOR...   DATE:

1.
2.
3.

I AM THANKFUL FOR...   DATE:

1.
2.
3.

I AM THANKFUL FOR...   DATE:

1.
2.
3.

START YOUR DAY WITH
———

GRATITUDE

MY WEEKLY GOALS ARE...

1. _____
2. _____
3. _____

I AM THANKFUL FOR...   DATE:

1. _____
2. _____
3. _____

I AM THANKFUL FOR...   DATE:

1. _____
2. _____
3. _____

I AM THANKFUL FOR...   DATE:

1. _____
2. _____
3. _____

"When you arise in the morning, think of what a precious privilege it is to be alive—to breathe, to think, to enjoy, to love—then make that day count!"

Steve Maraboli

I AM THANKFUL FOR...   DATE:

1.

2.

3.

I AM THANKFUL FOR...   DATE:

1.

2.

3.

I AM THANKFUL FOR...   DATE:

1.

2.

3.

I AM THANKFUL FOR...   DATE:

1.

2.

3.

START YOUR DAY WITH

GRATITUDE

MY WEEKLY GOALS ARE...

1. _____

2. _____

3. _____

I AM THANKFUL FOR...   DATE:

1. _____

2. _____

3. _____

I AM THANKFUL FOR...   DATE:

1. _____

2. _____

3. _____

I AM THANKFUL FOR...   DATE:

1. _____

2. _____

3. _____

> "Feeling gratitude and not expressing it is like wrapping a present and not giving it."
>
> **William Arthur Ward**

I AM THANKFUL FOR... DATE:

1.

2.

3.

I AM THANKFUL FOR... DATE:

1.

2.

3.

I AM THANKFUL FOR... DATE:

1.

2.

3.

I AM THANKFUL FOR... DATE:

1.

2.

3.

START YOUR DAY WITH

GRATITUDE

MY WEEKLY GOALS ARE...

1. _____

2. _____

3. _____

I AM THANKFUL FOR...   DATE:

1. _____

2. _____

3. _____

I AM THANKFUL FOR...   DATE:

1. _____

2. _____

3. _____

I AM THANKFUL FOR...   DATE:

1. _____

2. _____

3. _____

"Enjoy every moment of the journey, and appreciate where you are at this moment instead of always focusing on how far you have to go."

Mandy Hale

I AM THANKFUL FOR... DATE:

1.

2.

3.

I AM THANKFUL FOR... DATE:

1.

2.

3.

I AM THANKFUL FOR... DATE:

1.

2.

3.

I AM THANKFUL FOR... DATE:

1.

2.

3.

START YOUR DAY WITH

GRATITUDE

MY WEEKLY GOALS ARE...

1.
2.
3.

I AM THANKFUL FOR...   DATE:

1.
2.
3.

I AM THANKFUL FOR...   DATE:

1.
2.
3.

I AM THANKFUL FOR...   DATE:

1.
2.
3.

"Forget yesterday – it has already forgotten you. Don't sweat tomorrow – you haven't even met. Instead, open your eyes and your heart to a truly precious gift – today."

Steve Maraboli

I AM THANKFUL FOR... DATE:

1.

2.

3.

I AM THANKFUL FOR... DATE:

1.

2.

3.

I AM THANKFUL FOR... DATE:

1.

2.

3.

I AM THANKFUL FOR... DATE:

1.

2.

3.

GRATITUDE

MY WEEKLY GOALS ARE...

1.

2.

3.

I AM THANKFUL FOR...   DATE:

1.

2.

3.

I AM THANKFUL FOR...   DATE:

1.

2.

3.

I AM THANKFUL FOR...   DATE:

1.

2.

3.

"Let us be grateful to the people who make us happy; they are the charming gardeners who make our souls blossom."

Marcel Proust

I AM THANKFUL FOR... DATE:

1.

2.

3.

I AM THANKFUL FOR... DATE:

1.

2.

3.

I AM THANKFUL FOR... DATE:

1.

2.

3.

I AM THANKFUL FOR... DATE:

1.

2.

3.

REFLECTION

TAKE THE TIME TO LOOK BACK OVER TO PAST WEEKS AND REFLECT ON WHAT YOU WERE THANKFUL FOR, THE WAY IT MADE YOU FEEL AND HOW YOU FEEL NOW! SET SOME NEW MONTHLY GOALS THAT WILL PUSH YOU TO BE THE BEST VERSION OF YOURSELF.

MY GOALS FOR THE MONTH ARE...

1. _____
2. _____
3. _____
4. _____
5. _____

WHAT HAVE I BEEN MOST GRATEFUL FOR...

_____
_____
_____
_____
_____
_____
_____
_____

Draw Something

START YOUR DAY WITH

GRATITUDE

MY WEEKLY GOALS ARE...

1.
2.
3.

I AM THANKFUL FOR...   DATE:

1.
2.
3.

I AM THANKFUL FOR...   DATE:

1.
2.
3.

I AM THANKFUL FOR...   DATE:

1.
2.
3.

> "Great things happen to those who don't stop believing, trying, learning, and being grateful."
>
> **Roy T. Bennett**

I AM THANKFUL FOR...   DATE:

1.

2.

3.

I AM THANKFUL FOR...   DATE:

1.

2.

3.

I AM THANKFUL FOR...   DATE:

1.

2.

3.

I AM THANKFUL FOR...   DATE:

1.

2.

3.

START YOUR DAY WITH

GRATITUDE

MY WEEKLY GOALS ARE...

1.

2.

3.

I AM THANKFUL FOR...   DATE:

1.

2.

3.

I AM THANKFUL FOR...   DATE:

1.

2.

3.

I AM THANKFUL FOR...   DATE:

1.

2.

3.

> "Gratitude enables you to be fearless, and to never shy away from reveling in every moment of your life."
>
> **Janice Anderson**

I AM THANKFUL FOR... DATE:

1.

2.

3.

I AM THANKFUL FOR... DATE:

1.

2.

3.

I AM THANKFUL FOR... DATE:

1.

2.

3.

I AM THANKFUL FOR... DATE:

1.

2.

3.

START YOUR DAY WITH

GRATITUDE

MY WEEKLY GOALS ARE...

1. _____
2. _____
3. _____

I AM THANKFUL FOR...   DATE:

1. _____
2. _____
3. _____

I AM THANKFUL FOR...   DATE:

1. _____
2. _____
3. _____

I AM THANKFUL FOR...   DATE:

1. _____
2. _____
3. _____

"Cultivate and nurture being grateful for every good thing that comes to you, and to give thanks continuously. Remembering that In daily life we must see that it is not happiness that makes us grateful, but gratefulness that makes us happy."

Angie Karan

I AM THANKFUL FOR...   DATE:

1.

2.

3.

I AM THANKFUL FOR...   DATE:

1.

2.

3.

I AM THANKFUL FOR...   DATE:

1.

2.

3.

I AM THANKFUL FOR...   DATE:

1.

2.

3.

START YOUR DAY WITH

GRATITUDE

MY WEEKLY GOALS ARE...

1.

2.

3.

I AM THANKFUL FOR...   DATE:

1.

2.

3.

I AM THANKFUL FOR...   DATE:

1.

2.

3.

I AM THANKFUL FOR...   DATE:

1.

2.

3.

"The more you are grateful for what you have the more you can live fully in the present. When you live in the present moment the greater you can build stepping stones for a brighter future."

Dana Arcuri

I AM THANKFUL FOR... DATE:

1.

2.

3.

I AM THANKFUL FOR... DATE:

1.

2.

3.

I AM THANKFUL FOR... DATE:

1.

2.

3.

I AM THANKFUL FOR... DATE:

1.

2.

3.

START YOUR DAY WITH

GRATITUDE

MY WEEKLY GOALS ARE...

1. _____

2. _____

3. _____

I AM THANKFUL FOR...   DATE:

1. _____

2. _____

3. _____

I AM THANKFUL FOR...   DATE:

1. _____

2. _____

3. _____

I AM THANKFUL FOR...   DATE:

1. _____

2. _____

3. _____

"Finding happiness should not be seen as finding a needle in a haystack. Happiness is within. Each day is a blessing that brings an abundance of happiness. Therefore, finding happiness should be like finding a gift in a stack of gifts."

Steve Maraboli

I AM THANKFUL FOR... DATE:

1.

2.

3.

I AM THANKFUL FOR... DATE:

1.

2.

3.

I AM THANKFUL FOR... DATE:

1.

2.

3.

I AM THANKFUL FOR... DATE:

1.

2.

3.

GRATITUDE

MY WEEKLY GOALS ARE...

1. _____

2. _____

3. _____

I AM THANKFUL FOR...   DATE:

1. _____

2. _____

3. _____

I AM THANKFUL FOR...   DATE:

1. _____

2. _____

3. _____

I AM THANKFUL FOR...   DATE:

1. _____

2. _____

3. _____

> "Piglet noticed that even though he had a Very Small Heart, it could hold a rather large amount of gratitude."
>
> **A.A. Milne, *Winnie-the-Pooh***

I AM THANKFUL FOR...   DATE:

1.

2.

3.

I AM THANKFUL FOR...   DATE:

1.

2.

3.

I AM THANKFUL FOR...   DATE:

1.

2.

3.

I AM THANKFUL FOR...   DATE:

1.

2.

3.

GRATITUDE

MY WEEKLY GOALS ARE...

1. _____
2. _____
3. _____

I AM THANKFUL FOR...   DATE:

1. _____
2. _____
3. _____

I AM THANKFUL FOR...   DATE:

1. _____
2. _____
3. _____

I AM THANKFUL FOR...   DATE:

1. _____
2. _____
3. _____

> "I think that real friendship always makes us feel such sweet gratitude, because the world almost always seems like a very hard desert, and the flowers that grow there seem to grow against such high odds."
>
> **Stephen King, *The Eyes of the Dragon***

I AM THANKFUL FOR...   DATE:

1.

2.

3.

I AM THANKFUL FOR...   DATE:

1.

2.

3.

I AM THANKFUL FOR...   DATE:

1.

2.

3.

I AM THANKFUL FOR...   DATE:

1.

2.

3.

START YOUR DAY WITH

GRATITUDE

MY WEEKLY GOALS ARE...

1.
2.
3.

I AM THANKFUL FOR...   DATE:

1.
2.
3.

I AM THANKFUL FOR...   DATE:

1.
2.
3.

I AM THANKFUL FOR...   DATE:

1.
2.
3.

"We can always find something to be thankful for, and there may be reasons why we ought to be thankful for even those dispensations which appear dark and frowning."

Albert Barnes

I AM THANKFUL FOR... DATE:

1.

2.

3.

I AM THANKFUL FOR... DATE:

1.

2.

3.

I AM THANKFUL FOR... DATE:

1.

2.

3.

I AM THANKFUL FOR... DATE:

1.

2.

3.

COME TOGETHER IN

REFLECTION

TAKE THE TIME TO LOOK BACK OVER TO PAST WEEKS AND REFLECT ON WHAT YOU WERE THANKFUL FOR, THE WAY IT MADE YOU FEEL AND HOW YOU FEEL NOW! SET SOME NEW MONTHLY GOALS THAT WILL PUSH YOU TO BE THE BEST VERSION OF YOURSELF.

MY GOALS FOR THE MONTH ARE...

1. _____

2. _____

3. _____

4. _____

5. _____

WHAT HAVE I BEEN MOST GRATEFUL FOR...

_____

_____

_____

_____

_____

_____

_____

_____

Draw Something

START YOUR DAY WITH

GRATITUDE

MY WEEKLY GOALS ARE...

1. _____

2. _____

3. _____

I AM THANKFUL FOR...   DATE:

1. _____

2. _____

3. _____

I AM THANKFUL FOR...   DATE:

1. _____

2. _____

3. _____

I AM THANKFUL FOR...   DATE:

1. _____

2. _____

3. _____

> "Let me encourage you to get up every day and focus on what you do have in life. Be thankful for the blessings of the little things, even when you don't get what you expect."
>
> **Victoria Osteen**

I AM THANKFUL FOR...   DATE:

1.

2.

3.

I AM THANKFUL FOR...   DATE:

1.

2.

3.

I AM THANKFUL FOR...   DATE:

1.

2.

3.

I AM THANKFUL FOR...   DATE:

1.

2.

3.

GRATITUDE

MY WEEKLY GOALS ARE...

1. _____

2. _____

3. _____

I AM THANKFUL FOR...   DATE:

1. _____

2. _____

3. _____

I AM THANKFUL FOR...   DATE:

1. _____

2. _____

3. _____

I AM THANKFUL FOR...   DATE:

1. _____

2. _____

3. _____

> "As we express our gratitude, we must never forget that the highest appreciation is not to utter words but to live by them."
>
> **John F. Kennedy**

I AM THANKFUL FOR...   DATE:

1.

2.

3.

I AM THANKFUL FOR...   DATE:

1.

2.

3.

I AM THANKFUL FOR...   DATE:

1.

2.

3.

I AM THANKFUL FOR...   DATE:

1.

2.

3.

GRATITUDE

MY WEEKLY GOALS ARE...

1.

2.

3.

I AM THANKFUL FOR...   DATE:

1.

2.

3.

I AM THANKFUL FOR...   DATE:

1.

2.

3.

I AM THANKFUL FOR...   DATE:

1.

2.

3.

"When gratitude becomes an essential foundation in our lives, miracles start to appear everywhere."

Emmanuel Dalgher

I AM THANKFUL FOR... DATE:

1.

2.

3.

I AM THANKFUL FOR... DATE:

1.

2.

3.

I AM THANKFUL FOR... DATE:

1.

2.

3.

I AM THANKFUL FOR... DATE:

1.

2.

3.

START YOUR DAY WITH

GRATITUDE

MY WEEKLY GOALS ARE...

1. _____

2. _____

3. _____

I AM THANKFUL FOR...   DATE:

1. _____

2. _____

3. _____

I AM THANKFUL FOR...   DATE:

1. _____

2. _____

3. _____

I AM THANKFUL FOR...   DATE:

1. _____

2. _____

3. _____

> "Gratitude is the healthiest of all human emotions. The more you express gratitude for what you have, the more likely you will have even more to express gratitude for."
>
> **Zig Ziglar**

I AM THANKFUL FOR...   DATE:

1. _____
2. _____
3. _____

I AM THANKFUL FOR...   DATE:

1. _____
2. _____
3. _____

I AM THANKFUL FOR...   DATE:

1. _____
2. _____
3. _____

I AM THANKFUL FOR...   DATE:

1. _____
2. _____
3. _____